BAKER MAYFIELD
Feeling Dangerous

Andrew Gribble

The legend of Baker Mayfield began with his first NFL win, against the New York Jets 21–17 on Thursday Night Football, when he took the field in place of an injured Tyrod Taylor for his rookie debut.

Library of Congress Cataloging-in-Publication Data

Names: Gribble, Andrew author.
Title: Baker Mayfield : feeling dangerous / Andrew Gribble.
Description: Chicago, Illinois : Triumph Books LLC, [2019]
Identifiers: LCCN 2019020030 | ISBN 9781629377469
Subjects: LCSH: Mayfield, Baker, 1995– | Quarterbacks
    (Football)—United States—Biography. | Football
    players—United States—Biography. | Texas Tech Red
    Raiders (Football team)—History. | Oklahoma Sooners
    (Football team)—History. | Heisman Trophy—History.
    | Cleveland Browns (Football team : 1999–)—History.
    | National Football League—History. | Football—United
    States—History.
Classification: LCC GV939.B3455 G75 2019 | DDC 796.332092 [B]
    —dc23 LC record available at https://lccn.loc.gov/
    2019020030

This book is available in quantity at special discounts for your group or organization. For further information, contact:

Triumph Books LLC
814 North Franklin Street
Chicago, Illinois 60610
(312) 337-0747
www.triumphbooks.com

Printed in U.S.A.
ISBN: 978-1-62937-746-9
Design by Patricia Frey
Cover design by Preston Pisellini

Photos courtesy of AP Images unless otherwise indicated.

Contents

Defying the Odds from an
Early Age 6

Baker's Bold Decision 19

The Path to No. 1 32

Learning the Ropes 44

A Debut to Remember 55

Hitting His Stride While
Weathering the Storm 65

Cooking with Kitchens 76

"He Walk It Like He Talk It" 89

Right QB, Right Franchise 101

More Than a Quarterback 113

Defying the Odds from an Early Age

On the surface, Baker Mayfield grew up in the right place at the right time to become an NFL quarterback. He had football in his genes—a family that rooted him on at every single one of his Little League and Pop Warner games, a community that loved football as much as any in the United States, and a high school that was just beginning its unmatched stretch of cultivating Division I quarterbacks.

Still, Mayfield had to defy the odds. That's the only way he's known, and he's embraced it at every stop on his way to the instant NFL stardom he experienced as a rookie with the Cleveland Browns.

The son of James Mayfield—who was a quarterback and punter at the University of Houston—and Gina Mayfield, and the younger brother of Matt Mayfield—a walk-on for the Texas A&M baseball team—Baker Mayfield was born April 14, 1995, in Austin, Texas. It didn't take long for him to pick up the sports his dad and brother loved so dearly. When he was just three years old, Mayfield told his mother from that point on, he'd only watch ESPN.

Baseball, football, video games: those were Mayfield's passions, and his personal power rankings of the three depended on the day or year.

Don't be fooled by the first pitch Mayfield airmailed at a Cleveland Indians game shortly after the Browns drafted him in 2018. It all started with baseball, his first love. As early as the age of 10, Mayfield, a lefty at the plate, was his neighborhood's chief organizer of pick-up baseball tournaments, most of which would be headquartered in his own backyard.

As he does seemingly wherever he goes, Baker Mayfield took his opportunity to start at Lake Travis High School and ran with it, amassing 3,788 yards and 45 touchdowns in the 2011–12 season.

Had it not been for football, Mayfield perhaps could have made a career out of baseball.

He could play pretty much every position in the infield, starring as a shortstop and third baseman in his Little League years before settling in as a first baseman and designated hitter at Lake Travis High School. He earned Class 4A all-state honors after a junior season in which he batted .364, drove in 29 runs, and nearly led his team to a state title. Had it not been for football, Mayfield perhaps could have made a career out of baseball.

"Absolutely, he could have played in college. He could have played pro ball, as well," Daniel Castano, a former high school teammate of Mayfield's who went on to play baseball professionally, told Bleacher Report in a July 2018 article. That sentiment was echoed in the same article by Connor Mayes, another former teammate of Mayfield's who went on to play in the Royals' minor league system.

When Mayfield wasn't playing baseball or football under the scorching Texas sun,

he was in front of a TV next to his brother playing any variety of video games. When Nintendo 64 was the hottest system, it was non-stop battles of Hydro Thunder, Goldeneye and the latest version of NCAA Football, his brother told SoonerSports.com. By college, it was Halo 3, a popular Xbox game for which Mayfield has found time no matter how busy his schedule. He facetiously told teammates in high school he'd need to scale back on his football schedule to make time for the video game. At Oklahoma, his Halo 3 prowess became such a widely known skill that his own athletic department produced a longform feature on the subject. And just a few weeks after his rookie season, Mayfield sent out a tweet to his 515,000-plus followers to let them know "I'm back on Halo 3 like I never left."

The football field, though, was where Mayfield had the most staying power.

It all started in the fifth grade. Mayfield wanted to be a wide receiver. But his arm, as

In his junior year, Baker Mayfield led Lake Travis High School to its fifth straight Texas 4A state title.

he'd already shown for years on the baseball field, was too good to overlook at the game's most important position. Mayfield just took a little longer than most his age to grow into the role—literally. Mayfield's been undersized—compared to the average quarterback—throughout his career, but he was at an even bigger disadvantage as the players around him hit their growth spurts before he did. In a 2015 *Tulsa World* article, James Mayfield said Baker simply didn't play much as an eighth or ninth grader. By his own recollections, Mayfield was 5'2" and just 130 pounds when he finished middle school.

"Baker was still Baker, and he was throwing the ball better than the rest of them," James Mayfield told the *Tulsa World*. "He was just a little guy."

Mayfield, thanks to a long-awaited growth spurt, was creeping up on 6'0" by the time he joined the pipeline of quarterbacks at Lake Travis High, which was in the early stages of an extended run of sending its signal-callers to Division I schools (eight since 2006). Before there was Mayfield, there was Todd Reesing, a 2005 Lake Travis grad who went on to win an Orange Bowl at Kansas. There was Garrett Gilbert, one of the highest-ranked recruits in the nation in 2009 who led Lake Travis to two state titles and went on to play at Texas and SMU. Michael Brewer led the school to two

more state titles, then graduated in 2011 and enrolled at Texas Tech.

And then there was Collin Lagasse, a senior who beat out Mayfield, a junior at the time, for the starting job in 2011.

"I was disappointed. I'd worked so hard to get there but came up short. I felt like I'd failed at that time," Mayfield said in the docuseries *All the Way Up: Baker Mayfield*, which aired on FOX in July 2018.

"That's when I really looked myself in the mirror and said I'm going to keep working and whatever happens, happens. But when I get the opportunity to play, I'm going to take advantage."

The pecking order lasted just one possession into the 2011 season because Mayfield did just that.

Lagasse—whose athleticism was so impressive he wound up signing a scholarship to play wide receiver at SMU—separated his shoulder while scrambling on the fourth play of the game. That stroke of misfortune allowed Mayfield to take the job and run with it—a situation that would seemingly repeat itself wherever Mayfield went.

Playing before a raucous crowd of 35,000 at Darrell K Royal–Texas Memorial Stadium, Mayfield was unfazed. He threw for nearly 300 yards and ran for close to another 100 in the 35–7 victory over rival Westlake High.

A three-star recruit in the 2013 prospect class, Mayfield had some scholarship offers but chose to walk on at Texas Tech in the Big 12.

"By the way he came in and competed and really took control of the offense from Day 1, I had a feeling."

—KLIFF KINGSBURY ON BAKER MAYFIELD

The rest of the season was more of the same, with stats that looked more like what you'd see in the video games Mayfield loved to play. He threw for 3,788 yards and completed 65 percent of his passes with 45 touchdowns and just five interceptions. More importantly, Lake Travis didn't lose a game on its way to its fifth straight Texas 4A state title.

The wins didn't come as easy the following year, but Mayfield was just as good. He was the District 15-5A MVP after throwing 22 touchdowns and just three interceptions as Lake Travis saw its streak of five consecutive state titles come to an end.

His journey to the NFL, though, had only just begun.

Mayfield, considered a three-star recruit and ranked the No. 42 pro-style quarterback in the 2013 prospect class, had some scholarship offers—they just weren't big enough for Mayfield's liking. He could have gone to Rice, New Mexico, or Florida Atlantic, but Mayfield had bigger dreams.

"I easily could've gone to a place like Florida Atlantic, but my dad pushed me to realize that my dream was to play somewhere big," Mayfield told ESPN.com in August 2016. "He was right."

After an extended flirtation with TCU ended without an offer, Mayfield decided to walk on at Texas Tech, a Big 12 school that had just handed the coaching reins to 33-year-old Kliff Kingsbury. The decision didn't sit well with Mayfield's high school coach, Hank Carter, who admitted in an ESPN.com article he "wasn't real fired up" about Mayfield going to a school where his former Lake Travis High teammate, Brewer, and Davis Webb, a true freshman, were both on scholarship. There'd be an open quarterback competition

In his freshman year with Texas Tech, Baker Mayfield played under then-33-year-old head coach Kliff Kingsbury, now head coach of the Arizona Cardinals.

to kick off a new era of Red Raiders football, and Mayfield was confident he'd win it—even though the other competitors had a full set of spring practices under their belts, among other advantages.

Mayfield made the nearly six-hour drive northeast to Lubbock in early July and went right to work—on the scout team. A back injury essentially removed Brewer from the competition, leaving Kingsbury to decide between his scholarship freshman and the spunky walk-on who had that intangible "it" factor to him.

Mayfield's practice performance and comfort level within Kingsbury's Air Raid system left the coach with no other choice. This was Mayfield's team.

"By the way he came in and competed and really took control of the offense from Day 1, I had a feeling," Kingsbury told USA Today. "He stepped in like he'd been operating it for three years. It was better than anything I could have expected from him."

Kingsbury's decision was a historic one. When Mayfield took the first snap in Texas Tech's season opener against SMU—pitting him against another Lake Travis alum in Gilbert—he became the first true freshman walk-on to start

In his first (and only) season at Texas Tech, Baker Mayfield completed 64.1 percent of his passes for 2,315 yards and 12 touchdowns. He added another three rushing scores, such as this one against Southern Methodist.

a season opener for a Bowl Championship Series (BCS) school. And Mayfield did what he always seems to do, taking a big moment and making it special. The Red Raiders never trailed as Mayfield threw for 413 yards and four touchdowns—and ran 11 yards for another—en route to a 41–23 victory.

Mayfield was named the Big 12 Offensive Player of the Week just one week into his college career, but a knee injury he suffered a few weeks later added an extra layer of difficulty to his freshman season. Playing through pain in the majority of his eight games under center, he finished with 2,315 yards and 12 touchdowns. It was enough to make Mayfield the Big 12 Offensive Freshman of the Year, but it didn't get him the scholarship he coveted for the next semester.

"It was just different after I got hurt," Mayfield said in *All the Way Up: Baker Mayfield*.

"I've invested a lot into this and now you're telling me you don't have a scholarship for a guy who won five games after choosing to come here? That was the final straw for me."

It was time to go back to a place Mayfield knew almost as well as his hometown. ♦

He may have airmailed a ceremonial first pitch at a Cleveland Indians game in 2018, but Baker Mayfield's first love was baseball. He could play essentially every position in the infield and perhaps even could have gone pro.

Baker's Bold Decision

The thought first popped into Baker Mayfield's head during one of his lowest moments at Texas Tech.

Saddled with a knee injury, Mayfield stood on the sideline for the third consecutive week as he watched Davis Webb, the scholarship quarterback he'd beaten out for the job, run the show. The Red Raiders were undefeated— thanks mostly to Mayfield's performance in the first five games—but were up for their stiffest test yet at Oklahoma. It was a familiar place for Mayfield, who grew up an Oklahoma fan and spent a number of Saturdays tailgating outside the Palace on the Prairie before watching the Sooners take care of business.

Texas Tech fell to Oklahoma that day 38–30, its first of five consecutive losses to close out the 2013 season. By the time Texas Tech started its preparations for the Holiday Bowl, Mayfield was back in Austin plotting his next move.

It's one thing to think something. It's another to do it. Transferring to Oklahoma was possible, sure, but there were certainly easier paths available for Mayfield to resume his college career as a starting quarterback. Mayfield didn't care. It would have been easier to start right away at Florida Atlantic rather than walk on at Texas Tech, too.

Just days before Mayfield arrived on Oklahoma's campus, Trevor Knight looked like the next great Sooners quarterback in an upset victory over Alabama in the Sugar Bowl. Knight was a redshirt freshman with his whole career in front of him, and he'd just put up 348 yards and four touchdowns against an Alabama defense loaded with future NFL

After he transferred from Texas Tech to Oklahoma in 2014, the NCAA denied Baker Mayfield's waiver request to play immediately. Even so, he dazzled, going 9-of-9 for 125 yards and two touchdowns in Oklahoma's 2014 spring game and earning scout team offensive player of the year honors.

"He was a team guy. He hustled, busted his butt no matter what he was doing. Players respect that."

—Bob Stoops on Baker Mayfield

players. And there were four—yes, four- more quarterbacks behind Knight who would vie for the starting job when practice resumed in the spring.

Mayfield was undeterred. He confirmed his enrollment at Oklahoma to reporters on January 9 and met legendary coach Bob Stoops for the first time at a Sooners team meeting shortly thereafter. Stoops later called it "maybe the strangest thing that's ever happened in my coaching career."

Mayfield walked up to Stoops, introduced himself, and laid out his intentions. Stoops welcomed him with open arms, vowing to give Mayfield "every opportunity" to be the quarterback—just like everyone else in the crowded position group.

The NCAA denied Mayfield a chance at competing for the job in 2014, blocking his waiver request to play immediately despite transferring within the conference. It didn't stop him from leaving a lasting impression on his coaches and teammates. His performance in Oklahoma's 2014 spring game was nothing

short of perfect, as he completed all nine of his pass attempts for 125 yards and two touchdowns. And though he couldn't play on Saturdays, Mayfield made his mark during the week as the scout team quarterback, emulating the opponent's starter to help prepare Oklahoma's defense. He was an easy choice for Oklahoma's scout team offensive player of the year.

"Everybody saw it," Stoops said in *All the Way Up: Baker Mayfield*.

"He was a team guy. He hustled, busted his butt no matter what he was doing. Players respect that."

* * *

Before Mayfield's dream came true at Oklahoma, he had to weather a nightmare.

In late April 2015, Mayfield's mother, Gina, and his aunt, Kristi Brooks, were involved in a serious car accident in South Carolina that left three dead, including the driver of their car, Adrienne Davis. A seatbelt helped saved Gina's life, but left her with serious injuries

Trevor Knight (right) entered the 2015 season as the Sooners' returning starter, with four other quarterbacks behind him when Baker Mayfield entered the picture. But in practices, Mayfield showed coach Bob Stoops he was the man for the job and was named starter a week before the season opener.

to her abdomen. More than a month passed before she could return to Austin, but she was in a better place by the time Mayfield was back in Norman competing for the starting job.

"She had to kick me out of the house to do it," Mayfield said in his docuseries. "Once I got there, it was straight business."

Knight was the returning starter, but nothing was guaranteed for him after he labored through one of the worst Oklahoma seasons in years. For just the third time since 2005, the Sooners failed to win at least 10 games, finishing 8–5. The competition was wide open, and Mayfield took care of business from the moment practices opened in early August. A week out from Oklahoma's season opener against Akron, Stoops made it official.

"I could see a vision in my head that I'd play here eventually," Mayfield said shortly after he was informed of the decision. "It's a dream come true for me."

Mayfield's first official pass as a Sooner went 15 yards to Jarvis Baxter. The rest of his throws in a nearly spotless debut were just as good, and Oklahoma was rolling with their new leader at quarterback, who set a program record for most passing yards in a season opener.

It didn't take long for Mayfield to deliver one of his signature comeback victories. The very next week at Tennessee, Oklahoma trailed 17–3

Baker Mayfield's first statement game of his Sooners career came early, in Week 2 of the 2015 season. Oklahoma defeated Tennessee 34–21 in double overtime, with Mayfield rushing for a touchdown late and passing for three more.

"The relationships I built with some of those guys...I have best friends on that 2015 team that I'll have for life."

—Baker Mayfield on his Sooners teammates

entering the fourth quarter. Mayfield had two interceptions and not even 100 passing yards, but it mattered little when the game was on the line. He led the Sooners on back-to-back lengthy touchdown drives, capping the second with a touchdown pass to Sterling Shepard with 40 seconds to play to send the game to overtime. Mayfield ran for a touchdown in the first overtime and threw an 18-yard touchdown in the second to stun the 100,000-plus Tennessee fans who expected to rattle the first-year signal-caller.

A midseason loss to Texas gave Mayfield and the Sooners a dose of adversity, but they rallied back even stronger to finish the season playing as good of football as anyone in the country. Oklahoma held on for a victory against TCU in a game that saw Mayfield sidelined for the entire second half with a head injury and made it look easy in

the season finale at No. 11 Oklahoma State. Mayfield's 180 passing yards, 77 rushing yards, and three touchdowns powered the Sooners to a 58–23 rout and secured them a spot in the College Football Playoff. That's where the season would end, though, as Mayfield threw for 311 yards with a touchdown and two interceptions in the No. 4 Sooners' 37–17 loss to No. 1 Clemson in the Orange Bowl semifinal.

But Mayfield was just getting started.

"Looking back on the 2015 season, I was a good player, but, wow, did I make a lot of mistakes," Mayfield said in his docuseries. "I was just excited to play ball again. I always played fearless, but kind of played careless with my body.

"The relationships I built with some of those guys...I have best friends on that 2015 team that I'll have for life."

The Red River Rivalry game against Texas in 2015 provided Baker Mayfield with some adversity in his first year as Oklahoma's starter. Texas defeated Oklahoma 24–17, but it was the only game the Mayfield-led Sooners would drop in the regular season.

On June 1, 2016, Mayfield was told he'd have just one year of eligibility left when the Big 12 voted down a policy that would have given back the year of eligibility Mayfield lost when he transferred from Texas Tech. But 24 hours later, Big 12 faculty representatives, in a 7–3 vote, passed an amended policy that returned his eligibility, officially making him a junior entering the 2016 season.

Behind the scenes, it was a whirlwind 24 hours for Mayfield, who felt he was just getting started at Oklahoma. Publicly, Mayfield offered up a simple tweet shortly after the good news arrived.

"And y'all thought you were getting rid of me ..." he wrote.

Oklahoma was the No. 3 team in the country entering 2016, but it took just three weeks for the team's playoff hopes to be dashed. Mayfield picked up where he left off, throwing for 323 yards and two touchdowns, but the Sooners ran into a buzzsaw at Houston and lost their season opener. Two weeks later, in a highly anticipated showdown with Ohio State, Mayfield played one of his worst games at Oklahoma, and the No. 3 Buckeyes pounced on every opportunity in an absolute rout.

This was a turning point for Mayfield and the Sooners. He realized it in the moments right after the loss, making a pledge in his opening statement to reporters.

"We haven't played a Big 12 game yet, and I'm going to work harder than anyone in this program," Mayfield said. "I'm going to work harder than anyone Coach Stoops has ever seen."

The Sooners didn't lose another game. Mayfield and the entire Oklahoma offense clicked to the tune of 47.7 points per game in nine straight Big 12 wins that were rarely close. The unit's efficiency peaked in an instant

Above: In his first season starting for the Sooners, Baker Mayfield led them to the College Football Playoff. But that's where their ride would end that year, as Oklahoma lost to Clemson in the Orange Bowl semifinal. Opposite: Baker Mayfield sported the Golden Hat trophy after Oklahoma defeated Texas 29–24 in the 2017 Red River Showdown.

classic against future NFL MVP Patrick Mahomes and Mayfield's former team, Texas Tech. While Mahomes threw for 734 yards and five touchdowns, Mayfield was the more efficient quarterback with 545 yards and seven touchdowns in a 66–59 victory.

"That was my 'Welcome back to Lubbock' moment," Mayfield would say two years later. "Weird things happen in Lubbock, Texas, on Saturday nights."

There was nothing weird about Mayfield's presence at the 2016 Heisman Trophy ceremony. After throwing for 3,965 yards and 40 touchdowns, Mayfield, who received 26 first-place votes, finished third behind Louisville's Lamar Jackson and Clemson's Deshaun Watson.

Mayfield had one more year to prove he was the best player, and he did just that as a senior.

* * *

Stoops' unexpected retirement in June 2017 added a touch of uncertainty to Mayfield's final season. The promotion of offensive coordinator Lincoln Riley, who worked closely with Mayfield the previous two seasons, maintained the kind of continuity Oklahoma coveted entering a national-championship-or-bust season.

A Week 2 rematch with Ohio State in Columbus gave Mayfield a national stage to show how far he and Oklahoma had come since the previous year's embarrassing loss in Norman. Not only did Mayfield get it, but he delivered it in dominating fashion, throwing for 386 yards and three touchdowns in a 31–16 victory that wasn't as close as the score indicated. Mayfield celebrated the result in grandiose fashion, sprinting around the Ohio Stadium field holding an Oklahoma flag before trying to plant it at midfield in the center of OSU's famous "Block O."

There was little question who would hoist the Heisman Trophy for the 2017 season, as Baker Mayfield earned 732 votes to become Oklahoma's sixth winner of the prestigious award.

Mayfield later apologized for letting his competitive juices get the best of him. By the time he arrived in Cleveland, where thousands of Buckeyes fans call home, Mayfield was able to smile and laugh about it.

"You guys forget that they came to Norman and whooped up on us [the previous year]," Mayfield said.

A midseason upset at Iowa State elevated the pressure as Mayfield stared down the final stretch of his college career. What followed were eight of his best games at Oklahoma. The stretch peaked with a career-best 598 yards against Oklahoma State and ended with a 41–17 rout of No. 11 TCU to clinch a second trip to the College Football Playoff.

There were plenty of Heisman moments for voters to choose from, and no one came close to Mayfield's body of work. He produced the highest passing efficiency rating in FBS history while throwing for a career-best 4,340 yards, 41 touchdowns, and just five interceptions. Mayfield took home 732 votes to claim the award in lopsided fashion and become Oklahoma's sixth Heisman Trophy winner. In an emotional speech, Mayfield fought back tears as he looked at his family, who had stood confidently by his side whenever the odds felt most stacked against him.

"There were times we had to move. You guys made sacrifice after sacrifice just so I could chase my dreams," Mayfield said.

"It's been a dream come true to play at OU. Although I grew up in Austin, Texas, I was always Sooner born and Sooner bred, and, like they say, when I die I'll be Sooner dead.

"It's been a dream for me." ♦

Baker Mayfield felt the love from fans when he helped lead the Sooners over the rival Oklahoma State Cowboys in November 2015.

The Path to No. 1

Baker Mayfield's 2018 started with a thud.

On a picturesque New Year's Day at the Rose Bowl, Mayfield's college career ended abruptly. The No. 2 Sooners took a 14-point lead into halftime over No. 3 Georgia only to see it wither away over the course of the second half and two overtimes. Mayfield was fantastic in the first half and even caught a touchdown pass on a trick play by the goal line. But the ball just wasn't in his hands all that much in the second half as Georgia stormed back. Sony Michel's 27-yard touchdown run in the second overtime made it official: Mayfield's time at Oklahoma was over.

"I can't believe it's over," Mayfield said. "It's been a wild ride."

It was time to hop on a new ride, and this one would be just as wild.

Within weeks, Mayfield was in Mobile, Alabama, for the 2018 Senior Bowl. It was a unique year for the annual event, which draws more than 100 of the game's top seniors. It's not often a quarterback of Mayfield's caliber participates in the game—most first-round quarterback prospects either don't qualify because they're underclassmen or simply decline—and he wasn't even the clear-cut favorite to be the highest pick on his

Baker Mayfield's college career ended abruptly with a loss to Georgia in the Rose Bowl. But, as always, the quarterback found a moment to acknowledge the fans who supported him along the way.

"There's one thing I know how to do, and that's win ball games."

—Baker Mayfield during the week of the Senior Bowl

own North Team roster. Wyoming's Josh Allen didn't have anywhere close to the success Mayfield had at Oklahoma, but he looked the part at 6'5" and 237 pounds and had a cannon for an arm. The scales tipped even more in Allen's favor after ESPN NFL draft expert Mel Kiper Jr. projected the Cleveland Browns to take Allen with the No. 1 pick in his first mock draft. Adding even more pressure to the week, Mayfield and Allen were coached by Denver Broncos staff, who were in the market for a new quarterback and held the No. 5 pick.

Mayfield, of course, was unfazed.

"Despite what has happened in college, despite what I've done, that doesn't matter. That's all out the window. I've got to start fresh," Mayfield said in an interview that week with Cleveland radio station 92.3 The Fan. "Right now, the label is a short guy with the measurable stuff they look at and say I can't play NFL QB. I'm going to try to prove them wrong.

"There's one thing I know how to do, and that's win ball games."

Mayfield won the week, too, and it went beyond what happened on the field during three practices and a brief appearance in the game. Late into the night throughout the week, Mayfield went through his first meetings with a number of teams looking for an upgrade at quarterback. These encounters were quick and more of the get-to-know-you variety, but they set the table for the kind of hard questions Mayfield was to expect in the months to come. The toughest ones centered on the two moments from the previous year Mayfield regretted most.

The first was a February arrest in Fayetteville, Arkansas, for public intoxication and disorderly conduct—charges that were ultimately resolved with $300 in fines, $160 in court costs, $483.20 in restitution, and 35 hours of community service. The second happened on the field during Mayfield's Heisman-winning senior season, when he made an inappropriate gesture to Kansas players during a 41–3 rout. The decision came with immediate consequences, as

It's rare for a first-round quarterback prospect to participate in the Senior Bowl, but Baker Mayfield did, raising his draft stock along the way.

In February 2018, Baker Mayfield won the Davey O'Brien National Quarterback Award, presented annually to the nation's best quarterback.

Mayfield was benched for the first quarter of Oklahoma's game against West Virginia and stripped of his captaincy.

Cleveland Browns general manager John Dorsey just happened to be in the stands that afternoon in Kansas. Months removed from the end of his tenure as general manager of the Kansas City Chiefs, Dorsey wanted to be prepared for his next opportunity. For months, he watched film in his basement throughout the week and attended games whenever he could. Dorsey landed the job with the Browns in early December 2017 and inherited a treasure trove of draft assets but a mess at quarterback. The Browns held the No. 1 and No. 4 picks in the draft and were all but guaranteed to use one of the selections on a quarterback.

From the moment he arrived at the Senior Bowl, Dorsey showed an open mind and sense of humor about the mistakes Mayfield made in his past.

"He made the fans of Kansas upset, I can tell you that," Dorsey said during Mayfield's first Senior Bowl practice.

Dorsey later joked that he vetted Mayfield's arrest so much that he knew what the quarterback ordered from a food truck moments before the incident occurred. Clearly, Mayfield came into the pre-draft process carrying a clean slate with the team that held all the cards, and he aced the first part of the test.

"He demonstrated he was mature beyond his age," Dorsey would say a year later. "He demonstrated he truly is a galvanizer of people. He does that in his own way. He loves the game of football and he's ultra-competitive. You can't take that away from him."

Mayfield made the rounds at Super Bowl LII, doing countless interviews with radio shows, podcasts, and TV shows from coast to coast. The same questions came up, and Mayfield handled them with poise every time. After a few weeks of training in Los Angeles, his new offseason home, Mayfield was ready for everything the NFL was willing to throw at him at its ultimate, annual job fair: the combine. This was when Mayfield could truly unleash his inner competitive spirit.

Quarterback classes don't get much deeper than the one in which Mayfield found himself. In addition to himself and Allen, there were USC's Sam Darnold and UCLA's Josh Rosen—two prototypically built quarterbacks with all of the coveted characteristics who were eyed as future NFL starters before they even enrolled in college. From the moment Rosen arrived at UCLA and earned the starting job as a true freshman, NFL draft analysts pegged him as a first-round prospect. And from the moment Darnold, as a redshirt freshman,

delivered an electrifying performance against Penn State at the 2017 Rose Bowl, fans of teams poised to pick first in the 2018 NFL Draft embraced the catch phrases "Suck for Sam" or "Tank for Darnold" in hopes of landing the No. 1 pick.

Mayfield didn't care. He wanted to go No. 1, and he wasn't ashamed to admit it. He "absolutely" believed he was the best quarterback of the bunch and "if you don't have that mindset, then something's wrong." And when it came to Cleveland, Mayfield showed he'd clearly done his homework.

"First things first, they'd get a winner," Mayfield said. "If anybody's going to turn that franchise around, it'd be me. They're close, they're very close. They have the right pieces. They just need that one guy at quarterback to make that difference."

Two more meetings with the Browns ensured Mayfield would get his wish.

The first came where Mayfield was most comfortable, back in Norman on Oklahoma's campus. Timing prevented Dorsey and Cleveland's full scouting cavalcade to watch Mayfield at his Pro Day, which was scheduled on the same day free agency opened in the NFL. A few weeks later, Dorsey and a number of Cleveland's top executives, including head coach Hue Jackson, put Mayfield through a private workout. Mayfield looked the part on the field, but it was what happened away from

Baker Mayfield posed for a portrait at the NFL scouting combine on Friday, March 2, 2018.

In the final weeks and days leading up to the draft, it became unanimous. The Browns had their guy.

it that caught the eye of Jackson, who, a year earlier, said he preferred his quarterbacks to be 6'2" or taller.

"When we walked into the building, he made this sound. He just kind of came out of nowhere. He kind of went, 'Hee, hee!' And all the players in the building started going, 'Hee, hee!' And here they go. It's the most unbelievable thing I've ever seen," Jackson said a few days later at the NFL's spring league meeting in Orlando. "That shows you something about what he means to young men and how he leads them. And that's who Baker Mayfield is."

Mayfield got a chance to show even more members of the Browns organization who he was on a visit to the team's facility just a few weeks before the draft. He was the first of the top-billed quarterback quartet to visit, and he left a lasting impression.

"The one thing I realize when you get around him, he loves the game of football.

He loves to study football. He loves to play football," Dorsey said. "He is probably one of those guys as a young man he tried to compete at every sport and he wanted to be the best that he possibly could be."

Freddie Kitchens had been on the job as Browns running backs coach for a little more than two months when he first met Mayfield. The encounter was short, but Kitchens, who worked closely with quarterbacks Kurt Warner and Carson Palmer in his past positions with the Arizona Cardinals, saw all he needed to see.

"You get a sense when you are around him, there is just something," Kitchens said. "Coach [Bill] Parcells taught me a long time ago, the best instinct that you have is what your gut is telling you about a person, yea or nay. Just go with your gut. He is definitely one of those guys that you would say, 'Hey, man, I want to be around that guy.'"

Baker Mayfield impressed at the NFL combine, both in his on-field performance and in the answers he gave to some tough interview questions.

In the final weeks and days leading up to the draft, it became unanimous. The Browns had their guy. Nearly a year later, Dorsey admitted it was a decision he'd neared before he even accepted the job in Cleveland. He just wanted those closest to him to arrive to the same conclusion on their own.

"When you make a decision, you accumulate as much information as you can. But at the end of the day, you do not want to influence the room, you want to the room to have Baker earn their respect," Dorsey said. "I think he did that beyond the organization."

Dorsey played his cards close to the vest to the very end. So it should be filed under "pure coincidences" that Mayfield, in a tribute to a quarterback he idolized as a child, recreated the infamous photo of Brett Favre's draft day from 1991—all the way down to the jorts. Dorsey worked in the Packers scouting department for all but one of Favre's 16 seasons in Green Bay.

The photo, which went viral immediately, was more than just a way for Mayfield to win the Internet one day before the draft. It symbolized the tight bond Mayfield shared with his family and friends throughout his improbable journey and helped explain why he preferred to watch the draft from home rather than onsite at AT&T Stadium in Arlington, Texas.

"I want to be with my family, the people who helped me get to this point and celebrate with them. That's what it's all about," Mayfield said in a nine-part web series called *Behind Baker*.

"It's never been a one-man show."

Surrounded by seemingly every one of those people, Mayfield, still completely unaware of where he'd be headed, sat in his living room as the draft was about to begin. The room fell silent as Mayfield's phone rang. Dorsey was on the other end.

"Let me ask you a question," Dorsey said. "Do you want to be the first pick in the draft?"

"Yeah I do," Mayfield said.

"Well, buddy boy, I want you to get excited here. I'm going to put the card in here and we're going to take you with the first pick in the draft."

Tears welled in Mayfield's eyes as he chatted briefly with Jackson. When Mayfield hung up, the room erupted.

Hours later, Dorsey was asked if Mayfield reminded him of any other quarterback he'd been around in his decades of scouting and evaluating players. Perhaps the Hall of Famer Mayfield honored one day earlier?

"I see Baker Mayfield in Baker Mayfield," Dorsey said. ♦

The Cleveland Browns welcomed their No. 1 overall pick, Baker Mayfield, in a press conference shortly after the draft. Mayfield didn't attend the event, choosing instead to be home in Austin, Texas, with his family and friends.

Learning the Ropes

Some quarterbacks try to say all the right things, especially when they're on the big stage at the NFL Combine. That's what quarterbacks are supposed to do, right?

Baker Mayfield opted not to sugarcoat anything he said during a 15-minute session with reporters on a sunny Friday afternoon in early March.

"First things first, whatever team I go to, I'm not going to settle for a backup job. I've never been like that and I never will. I'm going to push that person in front of me," Mayfield said. "What it comes down to is the best man's going to win, I know that, but everybody has a role on the team and if you're not pushing those guys around you to be better, you're not doing it right."

One week later, the Cleveland Browns agreed to terms on a trade with the Buffalo Bills, sending a third-round pick in exchange for Tyrod Taylor, a veteran quarterback who made a Pro Bowl in 2015 and won more games than he lost in three seasons as the Bills' starter. Shortly thereafter, when he was introduced to the Cleveland media, Taylor was unequivocally named the starter of a team that saw five different starting quarterbacks combine to win just one game in the previous two seasons.

And then, of course, the Browns drafted Mayfield.

In the months since he made his comments at the Combine, Mayfield became well-versed in the Browns' plan for whichever quarterback they selected with the No. 1 pick. Both general manager John Dorsey—with Aaron Rodgers in Green Bay and Patrick Mahomes in Kansas City—and coach Hue Jackson—Carson Palmer

Baker Mayfield posed for a portrait during the NFLPA Rookie Premiere on Saturday, May 19, 2018.

in Cincinnati—had seen the benefits of a quarterback learning the complexities of the NFL game from the sidelines. And for a franchise that was in the process of turning over 60 percent of its roster, a veteran at the game's most important position was viewed as a much-needed stabilizer.

Understandably, it took just two questions into his post-draft conference call with local reporters for Mayfield to be reminded of his comments at the Combine.

"I know exactly what they said and exactly why they said that," Mayfield said. "That is a veteran that has been in the league, a guy that I can sit behind and learn from. When I say those types of things, it is because I am competitive. If I came in with the mindset of just being happy that I got drafted and just to settle for a backup job, that wouldn't be myself. I am going to come in and compete but also with the hunger to learn from a guy that has been in the league that has seen things that I haven't seen."

Taylor was an inspiration of sorts to Mayfield as he went through his career at Oklahoma. When he heard the naysayers proclaim he was too short to play quarterback at the next level, Mayfield often pointed to a handful of successful ones who took care of business while standing no taller than 6'1". Taylor just happened to be the first name off Mayfield's lips—followed by Russell Wilson and Drew Brees—when he went through that line of questioning at the Combine. Now, months later, Mayfield was backing him up.

A crowded quarterback room welcomed Baker Mayfield to the Browns. By the end of the preseason, he slotted in second in the pecking order, behind starter Tyrod Taylor and ahead of journeyman Drew Stanton.

Any potential awkwardness was wiped away by a mutual respect between the two.

"He is just an unbelievable guy," Mayfield said. "You see that, then you see him up here and actually how much he is up here, it is very transparent of who he is."

One year after they entered a season without a quarterback who had won a single NFL game, the Browns doubled down on experience with the signing of Drew Stanton. The 12-year veteran had the unique distinction of not only backing up talented young quarterbacks, but also talented young quarterbacks who were selected No. 1 in the draft. Before Mayfield, Stanton spent time with Palmer, Matthew Stafford, and Andrew Luck. Stanton's presence would allow Taylor to focus on all the responsibilities that come with being the starter and give Mayfield another "true professional" from which to learn. He also put Mayfield to work, commissioning the rookie to rent an RV for the quarterbacks to use as a getaway of sorts during the grind of training camp.

The group came together quickly, generating enough positivity for offensive coordinator Todd Haley, who'd worked closely with Hall of Famer Kurt Warner and future Hall of Famer Ben Roethlisberger in his previous stops, to label it "probably one of the best—if not the best—quarterbacks rooms, in general, that I've had."

The environment was right, and Mayfield thrived in it.

When he participated at the Browns' rookie minicamp a week after the draft, Mayfield showed plenty of zip and accuracy with his passes, but

Baker Mayfield shined in his rookie preseason debut against the New York Giants, throwing for 212 yards and two touchdowns, including one to tight end David Njoku (left).

Mayfield looked like a natural in Cleveland's offense, and the second-team group he led hummed with an efficiency unseen for years at Browns camp.

struggled a bit with exchanges under center. Granted, he was working mostly with players who would never crack an NFL roster, but this would be an adjustment for Mayfield, who largely worked out of the shotgun in high school and college.

"We are going to hammer that until I am good and it feels natural," Mayfield said.

By the time training camp opened, it was a non-issue. Mayfield looked like a natural in Cleveland's offense, and the second-team group he led hummed with an efficiency unseen for years at Browns camp. He formed a clear rapport with fellow rookie Antonio Callaway—a fourth-round pick with first-round talent who fell in the draft because of off-field concerns—and third-year possession receiver Rashard Higgins, who was fighting

to make the 53-man roster. Mayfield had his share of rookie moments at his first training camp, sure, but he showed marked improvement with each passing day.

He looked ready for more, but the Browns were steadfast in their plan to keep Mayfield behind Taylor—so much so that Mayfield didn't receive a single practice snap with the first-team offense. It didn't hurt that Taylor was having a great camp of his own. Even with HBO's *Hard Knocks* cameras covering every move, the prospect of a competition between Mayfield and Taylor was largely a non-story. While the three other early first-round quarterbacks—Sam Darnold with the Jets, Josh Allen with the Bills, and Josh Rosen with the Cardinals—had their every move and throw documented during open competitions,

In his last rookie preseason action, with then-offensive coordinator Freddie Kitchens calling the plays, Baker Mayfield looked like a seasoned pro. But he finished the game not knowing when he'd next see the field.

Before Browns training camp opened in 2018, Baker Mayfield accepted the ESPY for Best College Athlete for his time at Oklahoma.

Mayfield, as the No. 1 pick, somehow hummed under the radar.

"I'm here, working for the Cleveland Browns," Mayfield said. "If I was worried about that, then I wouldn't be focused, so I'll handle my business here.

"I have always had a one-day-at-a-time mindset. For me, I do have that sense of urgency to get better. Every opportunity I can get, I need to seize that day. For me, it is about taking it one day at a time, making sure that I am getting better every day."

Mayfield certainly seized the opportunities he received in the preseason, and it started with his debut against the New York Giants. He had a tough act to follow after Taylor was a perfect 5-for-5 with 99 yards and a touchdown, but Mayfield shined in his own way. His first touchdown throw showed off his patience in the pocket, as he waited and waited before floating a pass to tight end David Njoku, who snatched the ball between two defenders. Late in the fourth quarter, Mayfield fired a perfectly placed pass to a slanting Callaway on a third-and-4, who sprinted the rest of the way for a 54-yard touchdown.

Perhaps what stood out more than his numbers—11-of-20, 212 yards, two touchdowns—was Mayfield's comfort level and overall demeanor. He wasn't nervous—at least not noticeably—and the clips of him talking to players inside the huddle, which were captured by the *Hard Knocks* cameras

Mayfield certainly seized the opportunities he received in the preseason, and it started with his debut against the New York Giants.

and microphones, depicted Mayfield as being as carefree and confident as he was all those years ago in his parents' backyard.

"This is kind of fun, I'll be honest," Mayfield said at one point in the game.

After a couple of preseason performances that didn't go as smoothly, Mayfield made the most of what was viewed as his last action for the foreseeable future in Cleveland's preseason finale against the Detroit Lions. With running backs coach Freddie Kitchens calling the plays, Cleveland scored on its first three possessions and raced to a 25–0 first-half lead with Mayfield under center as the starter. He finished 9-of-16 for 138 yards, but the stats didn't reflect the ease in which Mayfield operated the offense. He looked ready, felt ready, but exited Ford Field unsure of when he'd next see the field.

"I'm ready to go. It's my job to be ready for that," Mayfield said after the game. "Any opportunity I can get, I'll take it. I'll be ready to do whatever it is, prepare the defense and just be ready to play as well."

★ ★ ★

In the days before that preseason finale, Mayfield was called into Jackson's office to be informed he would be the team's backup quarterback—ahead of Stanton—for the 2018 season. Months later, when he was asked to recount that moment and the irony of it considering what followed, Mayfield showed no hard feelings. He was able to understand the process while maintaining the competitive fire that never stops burning inside of him.

"They had a plan. They told me that before even the draft, before I even knew I was going there," Mayfield said in an interview on FS1's *Undisputed*.

"They asked me how I feel about it. Obviously, I want to play; that's who I am."

He played, all right, and he didn't have to wait all that long. ♦

A Debut to Remember

In back-to-back weeks, the Browns captivated the NFL world as they came oh-so-close to snapping the league's longest winless streak.

In Week 1, the Browns went the full 70 minutes in a driving rainstorm only to come away with a tie against the rival Pittsburgh Steelers. The next week, in New Orleans, Cleveland bottled up one of the NFL's most potent offenses. The Browns scored an improbable, game-tying touchdown in the final two minutes; but still came up short against the Saints 21–18 in a result mostly remembered for kicker Zane Gonzalez missing two extra points and two field goal attempts.

Baker Mayfield wasn't on the field for a single snap of it, and he wasn't anticipated to be when the Browns hosted the New York Jets for *Thursday Night Football*. And, really,

there wasn't even much of an outcry from fans for Mayfield to be given a chance against Jets rookie quarterback Sam Darnold, the No. 3 pick who won an open quarterback competition in the preseason and looked sharp in his NFL debut. Veteran Tyrod Taylor didn't look great in the first two games, by any means, but he came up big in the fourth quarter in each of them, leading a combined three touchdown drives in the game's final 15 minutes. The only question coach Hue Jackson faced regarding Mayfield in the days leading up to the game centered on Darnold, and whether the former USC star made the Browns' decision at No. 1 difficult.

"He is a fine prospect and is going to be a fine player. I think they got a good one," Jackson said of Darnold. "But we feel we have a really good one, too."

As he warmed up before the Browns' Week 3 game against the New York Jets, Baker Mayfield had no idea he would be called upon to finish it when starter Tyrod Taylor exited with an injury.

"I have to go do my job. Don't overthink it. Live in the moment. It's that time."

—Baker Mayfield on his NFL debut

The Browns found that out sooner rather than later in a situation that mirrored how Mayfield assumed the reins at Lake Travis High.

Taylor took hit after hit throughout a first half that was turning downright nasty at FirstEnergy Stadium. The Browns, favored to win at home for the first time since 2015, fell into a 14-point hole after back-to-back touchdowns from former Browns running back Isaiah Crowell. The atmosphere grew even more raucous when Crowell made a crude gesture after his second score before launching the ball into the stands. The fans were mad at him, sure, but they were just as mad at the team that had shown them so much hope in the first two games but, once again, looked like the same old Browns.

One play changed everything not just on this night, but for the rest of the 2018 season.

Facing yet another third-and-long, Taylor's head was driven into the turf when he was sacked by New York's Avery Williamson. The Browns punted, and Taylor was sent to the medical tent to be evaluated for a concussion. Mayfield got the tap on the shoulder to get ready, and within a couple of minutes, he was summoned to the huddle. Suddenly, the energy inside FirstEnergy Stadium flipped. As Mayfield jogged toward his teammates, the capacity crowd of 67,431 welcomed him with a standing ovation.

Mayfield, though, was undeterred. He engaged in a little smack talk with Jets defensive players, who were salivating at the prospect of facing a rookie in his NFL debut, and focused on the task at hand.

"Treat it like any other time," Mayfield said, recalling what he thought to himself as he stepped on the other side of the white lines. "I have to go do my job. Don't overthink it. Live in the moment. It's that time. I have to command the offense. I have to command the team. I have to bring a spark and give us a chance to win."

Before the game against the New York Jets that would become his NFL debut, Baker Mayfield met former Dallas Cowboys quarterback and current broadcaster Troy Aikman.

Mayfield stood a few yards behind center with running back Duke Johnson to his left as the Browns took over at their 34-yard line with 1:42 to play in the second quarter. Mayfield took the snap, dropped back three steps, and fired a strike to Jarvis Landry for a 14-yard gain. He did it again on the next throw, completing a 17-yarder to tight end David Njoku. His first NFL sack put him in a hole, but he crawled out of it with a 16-yard throw to Landry on the very next play. The drive stalled, but the Browns were on the board with a field goal to carry some momentum into a locker room that was already chock-full of Baker believers.

"It's just a testament to how he has worked since the day he stepped into this building and not having that backup mentality," Landry said. "He was so ready for this moment. He was prepared for this moment. He grabbed it by the horns."

The moment that symbolized this night truly belonged to Mayfield came with the quarterback in an unfamiliar spot. A seven-play, 69-yard touchdown drive, highlighted by Mayfield's 29-yard dart to Landry near the goal line, got the Browns within two late in the third quarter. For weeks, the Browns drilled their version of the "Philly Special," waiting for the right moment to unleash the goal-line play that put the ball in the hands of Landry and the quarterback in the corner of the end zone as a wide receiver. The only problem was Mayfield had never practiced it, because Taylor took every single snap.

Baker Mayfield couldn't contain his excitement after leading the Browns to a 21–17 victory against the New York Jets in his NFL debut, breaking a 19-game losing streak for the franchise.

Former Cleveland Browns left tackle Joe Thomas congratulated Baker Mayfield on his win on the set of Thursday Night Football after the Browns beat the New York Jets 21–17 in Week 3 of the 2018 season.

It was one regular season victory in the first month of the season, but it meant so much more for a franchise that had just one win in the previous two years and a mix of mediocrity and incompetence at the quarterback position since the team returned in 1999.

Mayfield had no choice but to learn it on the fly, and he didn't want that to affect the mindset of his teammates in such a crucial moment.

"He comes to me and says, 'Your ass better throw me that ball. No matter what,'" Landry said. "I said, 'I got you.'"

As the players around him settled into their positions, Mayfield stepped up to the left side of the line as if he were changing the play. The ball was directly snapped to Johnson, who quickly pitched it to Landry, a southpaw who immediately looked Mayfield's way. Mayfield was all alone in the corner of the end zone for the game-tying catch. Mayfield's swagger was immediately unleashed, as he held the ball out with his right hand, locked eyes with the fans and strutted for a few steps, providing

one of the more iconic images from his rookie season.

Still, there was more work to be done, especially after the Jets reclaimed the lead with a field goal with 8:56 left to play. Mayfield's first throw could have gone for 30 or more yards, but it was dropped by Antonio Callaway. Mayfield didn't lose a shred of confidence in his fellow rookie and went right back to him in a pivotal spot, facing third-and-10 at the Jets' 26. Mayfield fired an eight-yard throw to Callaway, who used his momentum to get the next two yards and pick up the first down. A Carlos Hyde touchdown run on the next play was nullified by a penalty, but Mayfield got the Browns right back inside the 10 with a 12-yard throw to Landry. Four plays later, the Browns scored on

a one-yard Hyde run and had their first lead of the game.

"That was a 15-play drive," Landry said. "That's incredible."

The Browns defense did the rest, intercepting Darnold on back-to-back possessions to seal the 21–17 victory. Most fans stayed in their seats for a few moments after the victory was sealed with a Mayfield kneel-down to soak up the moment. When they finally exited, they crowded the ramps, walking a little slower than usual in hopes this party wouldn't come to an end. Chants erupted, echoing above the streets outside of FirstEnergy Stadium and inside bars across Cleveland, where free beer was released from locked fridges as part of a Bud Light promotion.

"BA-KER MAY-FIELD!" *clap, clap, clap, clap, clap.*

It was one regular season victory in the first month of the season, but it meant so much more for a franchise that had just one win in the previous two years and a mix of mediocrity and incompetence at the quarterback position since the team returned in 1999. Longtime Browns beat reporter Tony Grossi called it "the most electrifying NFL debut for a Browns quarterback," and it was hard to find anyone who disagreed.

"Mayfield didn't do it alone," Grossi wrote on ESPNCleveland.com, "but he was the juice that lit up the night—and the future of a franchise lost in darkness for over a decade."

Landry knew what he saw. It wasn't just that Mayfield led the Browns to their first victory in the last 19 tries. It was how he did it and how the players around him elevated their performance because of his presence.

"I don't think there is a coach or a player in this building who has doubted him or felt like we were in a disadvantage when he came onto the field," Landry said. "That is something that you have to love about him.

"That is why he was the first pick. That is why he was the Heisman Trophy winner. You saw it tonight firsthand."

Jackson didn't let himself get caught up in the moment and declined to name Mayfield the permanent starter in the immediate aftermath of the victory. When the team returned from a long weekend, Jackson had made up his mind and promptly met with his quarterbacks.

This was Mayfield's team.

"The guy that we picked for the future of the organization is now the starter of the team," Jackson said.

"He put himself into the position to be a backup and in this game was able to play well. He nailed it." ♦

When Baker Mayfield took the field for an injured Tyrod Taylor in his NFL debut against the New York Jets, he recalls thinking to himself, "Don't overthink it. Live in the moment. It's that time."

Hitting His Stride While Weathering the Storm

Ten days and more than 2,500 miles separated Baker Mayfield from his dynamic, storybook NFL debut and his first NFL start. It was a journey to get to this point, so why not add a few more days and a cross-country flight to the mix?

Mayfield, though, wouldn't change a single thing about how he approached the upcoming game at Oakland. From the moment he arrived in Cleveland, Mayfield prepared as if he were the starter. Now, he simply was the starter, and there was no turning back.

"[I need to] be that same person like I have been from the second I walked in this building, and that is what they need to see," Mayfield said. "They need to see that I am not going to change no matter the circumstances—starter, backup or whether we are winning or losing. I am going to be that same person for these guys, and they can count on that."

Mayfield didn't really have a "Welcome to the NFL" moment in his near-spotless debut. Instead, it arrived a few minutes into his

Outwardly, Baker Mayfield seemed unfazed about making his first NFL start in Oakland against the Raiders in Week 4 of the 2018 season.

first start, when a pass intended for Antonio Callaway sailed a touch wide, grazing off the receiver's hands and into the waiting arms of Gareon Conley. By the time Mayfield chased to cut off Conley's angle, the Raiders cornerback was already in the end zone for a pick-six.

In the past, this would be a moment that would break most young Browns quarterbacks. One mistake would lead to two more. Then three more. Then all of a sudden, the game would be out of hand.

Mayfield, meanwhile, responded by leading three consecutive scoring drives. He capped the stretch with his first of many awe-inspiring throws of his rookie campaign, pump-faking before firing downfield to tight end Darren Fells. Mayfield put it where only the former international basketball player could get it, and Fells trotted in for a 49-yard touchdown. Mayfield celebrated his first NFL pass with two big fist-pumps, shouting "Boom!" each time as he hugged the offensive linemen around him.

However, the end of his first start just wasn't as storybook as the previous week. The Browns came up short in a back-and-forth overtime shootout that left Mayfield and Cleveland on the wrong end of a 45–42 result. Still, Mayfield, who threw for 295 yards and two touchdowns but was also responsible

Even though Baker Mayfield's first NFL start was a loss, there were plenty of highlight-reel moments as he led three consecutive scoring drives, including a touchdown pass to wideout Jarvis Landry.

for four turnovers (two interceptions, two fumbles), left another unmistakable impression.

"I think Cleveland found their quarterback," Raiders coach Jon Gruden said. "They have been complaining about not having one for a while, but it's pretty obvious they got one."

One week later, against the Baltimore Ravens, Mayfield showed what he was made of with his back against the wall.

Facing one of the NFL's perennially dominant defenses, Mayfield slogged through four quarters and managed to lead the Browns to just nine points. His 19-yard touchdown pass to Rashard Higgins near the end of the first half was the lone highlight. Fortunately, the Ravens mustered just nine points of their own, and the Browns were headed to their third overtime period in their first five games.

The Browns punted and turned it over on downs on their first two overtime possessions. The Ravens punted twice, the second of which set up Mayfield and the Browns at their own 16-yard line with 2:55 to play. Adding an extra degree of difficulty to the situation, Cleveland's first play from scrimmage, a reverse to wide receiver Rod Streater, lost 11 yards. It was second-and-21 from the 5-yard line against a Ravens team that hadn't let the Browns sniff any points since the first half. Game on the line.

The next two plays changed everything.

Facing a mess of trouble in the pocket, Mayfield escaped and picked up 13 of the most important rushing yards of his rookie season. On third-and-8, it got even messier, as Mayfield dropped back and saw nothing opening up in front of him. He waited and waited, with future Hall-of-Fame pass rusher Terrell Suggs charging his way, before dropping back a few more steps and firing a pass to Derrick Willies. The undrafted rookie wide receiver secured it at the first-down marker as his defender fell to the turf and bolted upfield for 39 yards. Three straight runs by Duke Johnson put the Browns in field goal range, and Greg Joseph knocked it through for the Browns' first division victory since Week 5 of the 2015 season. Mayfield was the ninth quarterback to start a game during that stretch.

"I haven't been around him a ton, but there is just something about this young man," Browns coach Hue Jackson said. "He has a feel to him. He doesn't blink at situations or opportunities. Something might have went wrong the play before, and it's water off of the duck's back to him."

The next three weeks would test that mentality more than ever.

With a chance to have a winning record for the first time since 2014, the Browns fell flat in Week 6 against the Chargers. Mayfield rolled his ankle on a scramble, took five

Baker Mayfield reunited with former Oklahoma teammates Orlando Brown Jr. (left) and Mark Andrews (middle) after the Browns defeated the Baltimore Ravens in Week 5 of the 2018 season.

sacks, threw two interceptions, and didn't get the Browns into the end zone until the early part of the fourth quarter. The next week against the Tampa Bay Buccaneers saw Mayfield get battered in the first half before rallying the Browns from a 14-point, fourth-quarter deficit to send the game to overtime. Given a golden opportunity at midfield after a Jamie Collins interception, the Browns offense went three-and-out and never got the ball back in another loss.

After just one win in Mayfield's first four NFL starts, frustration swirled around him, as the Browns trended toward another disheartening season, but Mayfield maintained his poise.

"We don't need to try to change too much," Mayfield said. "We just need to get better at what we are doing. There is not a secret recipe for success besides working your ass off with what you have."

Change, though, was right around the corner whether Mayfield liked it or not.

A midseason rematch with Pittsburgh quickly turned into a nightmare after the Browns raced out to a 6–0 lead. Pittsburgh scored the next 14 and absolutely dominated the second half en route to a 33–18 victory that wasn't as close as the score indicated. Mayfield was hit hard again, taking two sacks and seven quarterback hits. The Browns boarded their buses back to Cleveland with a 2–5–1 record and a second-half schedule that appeared

It didn't take Baker Mayfield long to start making a difference in the Cleveland community. He made sure to introduce himself to Dylan Sutcliffe, whom the Browns signed to a one-day contract in 2015 to make his dream of playing for the team come true. Sutcliffe suffers from ataxia telangiectasia.

to be even less forgiving than the first half. Mayfield lost just six times as a starter at Oklahoma. After five NFL starts, he had four. He was completing 58 percent of his passes with eight touchdowns and six interceptions.

This was the NFL giving the No. 1 pick the rude awakening it delivers to every player at some point during his rookie season. It just didn't knock this one down.

"I've seen better days," Mayfield said.

"We show flashes of a great offense. It's always one play here or there that stops us. That is the hope we have to keep consistency within that and continue to do those things. We'll see what happens. I'm fine with what we have."

Browns' ownership and general manager John Dorsey felt differently. Mayfield would enter the second half of his rookie season with a new head coach and an offensive coordinator who'd never called plays in a regular season NFL game. Shortly before noon the following Monday, Cleveland fired Jackson and offensive coordinator Todd Haley, citing a desire to rid the organization of any "internal discord" moving forward. Defensive coordinator Gregg Williams would take the reins as head coach, while running backs coach Freddie Kitchens would assume the role of offensive coordinator.

In the weeks leading up to his dismissal, Jackson, who also served as the team's offensive coordinator in the previous two seasons, expressed a desire to

Though he would scramble and rush for 131 yards his rookie season, the 13 yards Baker Mayfield picked up against the Baltimore Ravens in Week 5 to set up the game-winning field goal were perhaps his most important.

This was certainly a learning experience for Mayfield, but it wasn't a foreign one.

be more involved with the team's struggling offense. It never happened, and both were gone because of their inability to effectively collaborate. The last thing Dorsey and Browns ownership wanted was Mayfield's progress to be stalled because of it.

"Whenever you take your quarterback the No. 1 pick, you want to see him develop in that role," Dorsey said. "Now, we all know that all of a sudden you are a rookie quarterback and you are thrusted in five games early into the season as your starter. He is going to see very complex defenses, and it is not going to happen overnight. He is going to have his ups and downs, but he is going to learn along the way."

This was certainly a learning experience for Mayfield, but it wasn't a foreign one. Bob Stoops chose to leave Oklahoma on his own terms, but the decision came just a couple months before the start of Mayfield's senior season. It was abrupt in its own way, leaving Mayfield and the locker room he led to look inward as they eyed a season with sky-high expectations. The Sooners, of course, delivered with their second trip to the College Football Playoff.

"We used that to come together," Mayfield said. "I expect the guys in here to be grown men, to be experienced football players and to handle it that way and keep that same mindset of that we have the same goal."

Later in the interview, Mayfield was asked if he, as the No. 1 pick and future of the franchise, would be the player the team could count on to "pull the franchise up by its bootstraps." Mayfield nodded his head and delivered his shortest answer of the day.

"Bring it on." ◆

After getting out to a 2–5–1 record to start the season, the Browns organization decided it was time for a shakeup. Head coach Hue Jackson and offensive coordinator Todd Haley were out; defensive coordinator Gregg Williams (right) became Baker Mayfield's interim head coach.

Cooking with Kitchens

The Browns had just lost their fourth straight game, and the result wasn't all that close.

The Chiefs and their high-powered offense rolled into Cleveland with just one loss, punched the Browns early and never trailed en route to a 37–21 victory that would have been even worse if Kansas City kept its foot on the gas for the full 60 minutes. Cleveland was 2–6–1—not even a month removed from Mayfield's overtime heroics against the Ravens in a game that felt like a season-changing win—and all alone in the basement of the AFC North. In the coming days, ESPN and The Athletic would both publish articles questioning whether the Browns would win any of their remaining seven games.

Yet as Mayfield stood behind the podium in the immediate aftermath of his fifth loss as an NFL starter, he couldn't shake the positivity that flowed through him. This defeat felt different than the previous four. Cleveland's offense, under the guidance of first-time offensive coordinator Freddie Kitchens, did what it set out to do against the Chiefs, establishing long drives to milk the clock and punching in its red-zone opportunities. Kansas City was just too much to handle.

Months later, Mayfield, who threw for 297 yards and two touchdowns in the loss, would call this the turning point in his rookie season.

"I felt like we had them in the first half. It was really close," Mayfield said in a Super Bowl LIII Radio Row interview with ESPN. "We just had a few plays not go our way. Just to see we were competing at that time, the Chiefs were on a roll. Looking back on it, we realized at that point we have something here."

The Browns dealt with some adversity in the middle of Baker Mayfield's rookie season, dropping four consecutive games between Weeks 6 through 9.

"When I woke up this morning, I was feeling pretty dangerous."

—BAKER MAYFIELD IN A PRESS CONFERENCE

"That point in the season was really fun."

The fun, as Kitchens would later say, was in the winning. And Mayfield and the Browns would have a whole bunch of it over the next seven games.

It started with an open dialogue.

Mayfield never had any documented issues with former offensive coordinator Todd Haley. In fact, when questions swirled about Hue Jackson involving himself more with the offense, Mayfield was adamant wholesale changes weren't necessary. With Kitchens, though, Mayfield had a coach who knew what he didn't know. Thrust together with just six days to prepare for the Chiefs, Kitchens and Mayfield clicked by endlessly drilling the upcoming game plan. Communication was stressed to the highest degree, as Kitchens crowd-sourced his play sheet by asking Mayfield and other offensive players which plays they liked best and which ones they'd prefer to never run again. Each week under Kitchens, the offensive line filled out a notecard with its five favorite plays—a request list, of sorts, that would ultimately be a part of the game plan. The terminology of Haley's offense didn't change a lick, but the players—Mayfield, especially—felt empowered.

The breakthrough came Week 10 against the Falcons.

On a crisp, sunny Sunday at FirstEnergy Stadium, Mayfield played the most efficient game of his rookie season. He completed his first 13 passes and needed just 20 attempts in all to finish with 216 yards and three touchdowns in Cleveland's 28–16 victory. His quarterback rating of 151.3 was the best-ever by an NFL rookie who attempted a minimum of 20 passes. It was the fifth-best by any quarterback in Browns history and set the table for Mayfield's most memorable moment behind the microphones.

"When I woke up this morning, I was feeling pretty dangerous," Mayfield said, wiggling his eyebrows as the room filled

The Browns couldn't get the job done against the high-powered Kansas City Chiefs in Week 9, but then-offensive coordinator Freddie Kitchens and Baker Mayfield were proud of the way the new-look Browns executed their game plan nonetheless.

That tight bond made the tougher moments between Kitchens and Mayfield valuable instead of detrimental.

with laughter. "I just woke up feeling really dangerous."

That feeling turned into a common one throughout the rest of the season.

A bye week didn't halt Mayfield's momentum a single bit in Cleveland's Week 12 romp over the Bengals. The Browns scored touchdowns on their first four possessions, three of which ended with Mayfield touchdown passes, to storm out to a 28–0 lead. Mayfield threw his fourth—all four going to different players—early in the third quarter to set a season-best mark and allow the Browns to cruise to their first set of consecutive victories since 2014.

An icy postgame handshake between Mayfield and former Browns coach Hue Jackson, who quickly joined the Bengals as a special assistant after his firing, made plenty of headlines in the days following the win. Mayfield, who made a controversial comment about Jackson in an Instagram post one day after the game, drew the ire of some for his perceived poor sportsmanship, but it seemingly strengthened the bond between Kitchens and himself.

"I promise you this: Baker is not going to blow smoke up anybody's ass," Kitchens said. "If he said it, that is what he feels, and I am standing behind Baker Mayfield. I do not care about anyone who does not work in this building and what they think about what he said. That is what I stand behind, is him and the players in this locker room."

That tight bond made the tougher moments between Kitchens and Mayfield valuable instead of detrimental. Even though Mayfield's second half of 2018 was mostly one highlight after the other, there were still moments of adversity, moments when Mayfield could have been much better than he was.

When the Browns snapped their four-game losing streak in Week 10 against the Atlanta Falcons, Baker Mayfield couldn't help but record the ensuing celebration for posterity.

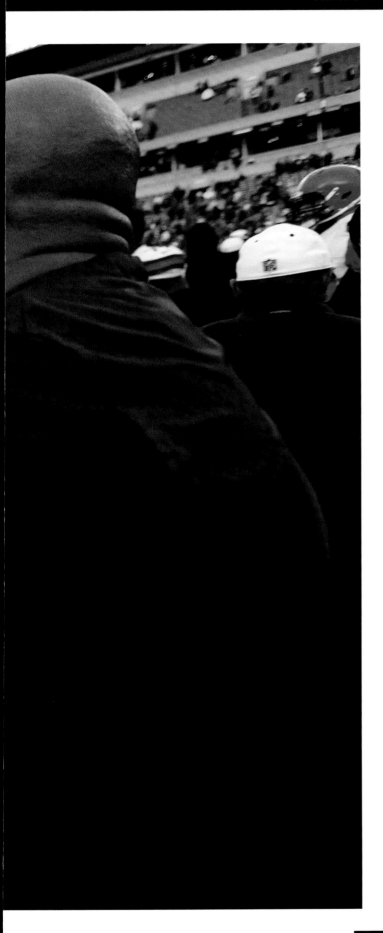

There was the first half against the Texans in Week 13. After two straight wins, the Browns were facing one of the league's best defenses in an opportunity to prove to doubters what they were building was real and sustainable. Mayfield threw his first interception in nearly a month in the first quarter and followed with two more before halftime. He rebounded with a historic second half, throwing for a whopping 351 yards in the final two quarters, but the Browns couldn't recover from their early struggles.

And then there was the Browns' primetime Saturday night matchup with the Broncos in Week 15, a showdown between two teams on the fringe of the playoff picture that essentially served as an elimination game for the loser. Mayfield came out hot, firing a pinpoint touchdown pass to Breshad Perriman on Cleveland's first offensive possession, but struggled to replicate that success over the next two quarters. He was trying to make the big play with each one of his throws instead of taking what the defense gave him. Kitchens let him know as much in frank fashion, and what followed was one of Mayfield's best moments of his rookie season. With the Browns on the cusp of taking the lead early in the fourth quarter, Mayfield flashed a smile as he eyed Denver's defensive

The postgame greeting between Baker Mayfield and his former head coach, Hue Jackson, after the Cleveland Browns defeated the Cincinnati Bengals in Week 12 was best described as "icy."

"Sometimes, they need confidence. But you have to tear away the façade and see what the kid needs and then you can get him better. And then, the relationship forms."

—Freddie Kitchens on Baker Mayfield

alignment. After identifying a mismatch to his left, Mayfield promptly audibled out of a running play, took the snap, and fired a pass to a slanting, wide-open Antonio Callaway. The Browns had the lead, and they never gave it back—on a night Mayfield further solidified his place as the franchise quarterback Cleveland had been longing for since the 1980s.

"You earn trust by talking and figuring out who the person is," Kitchens said. "When you tear away all of the façade, who is the person and what makes him tick? Once you get to know the person, it enables you to have tough conversations. Those tough conversations are the ones that end—those butt chewings— those are the ones that get them better.

"Sometimes, they need confidence. But you have to tear away the façade and see what the kid needs and then you can get him better. And then, the relationship forms."

By the end of the season, this tight-knit relationship was impossible to ignore. In a back-and-forth with reporters leading up to the Broncos game—and just a week removed from finding out Mayfield's and Kitchens' alma maters were squaring off in the Orange Bowl—Mayfield looked aghast when he was asked if he and Kitchens were "like-minded."

"I am not like-minded like Freddie. No, he is going down when it comes to the Orange Bowl. We are not like-minded at all. He is from Gadsden, Alabama," Mayfield said,

Baker Mayfield was all smiles in his postgame presser after the Browns put away the Denver Broncos in a primetime Week 15 game that essentially served as a playoff elimination game.

accentuating the last part with his best crack at a Kitchens impersonation.

A reporter clarified he was talking about their overall game-planning philosophies. Mayfield then struck a more serious tone about the connection he had with his play-caller.

"It has been great to be able to learn from him," Mayfield said.

"We have grown a lot and learned a lot since then and since we started playing under Freddie and having him call the plays."

Kitchens got his barbs in, too, joking that Mayfield got the headbands he wears on game days at Lululemon. And in the throes of Cleveland's lopsided, Week 16 victory over the Bengals, Kitchens approached Mayfield on the sidelines after he'd just led a touchdown drive and scratched his chin.

"That guy's an idiot," Mayfield said as Kitchens walked away.

Kitchens, though, was no dummy, and the impact he left on Mayfield and the players around him was impossible to ignore as the Browns embarked on their search for a new head coach. Kitchens, who'd been a position coach for 12 years before his sudden promotion to offensive coordinator midway through his 13th NFL season, was the last of seven candidates to interview. He was called back for a second interview the next day, the first of two to receive the invitation. Two days later, he was on the job as Cleveland's 17th full-time head coach.

Mayfield was thousands of miles away from Cleveland when the news landed. He had to trust the Browns would make the right decision, whoever got the job. Needless to say, the Browns didn't have to check on Mayfield to hear if he was happy with the decision.

"I kind of had that sense the whole time, just seeing how he was, how he didn't change when he jumped from running backs coach to offensive coordinator. Then, just taking over and the difference that we had when he was calling plays. You know what, he had guys believing in him," Mayfield said in an interview on SiriusXM's Mad Dog Sports Radio. "When you have guys believing in the head coach and respecting you, it's going to be great things that happen, so that was my choice, I believe in him.

"That's not to say anything about anybody else, but we had something special and I want to build on it." ♦

When the Browns announced Freddie Kitchens' promotion to head coach after the season, they knew their franchise quarterback would be pleased with the move.

"He Walk It Like He Talk It"

Baker Mayfield isn't for everybody. He knows that, and, frankly, he doesn't care.

"Although I'm an athlete, I'm not a cookie-cutter quarterback. I never have been, never will be. I speak my mind," Mayfield said midway through his rookie season. "People don't have to care. I'm not looking for anybody's approval."

What rubs some the wrong way—the charisma, the neverending confidence, the swagger, the dance moves, the headline-making quotes, the childlike giddiness he shows even in the NFL—has resonated in a big way with the teammates and coaches who have been a part of Mayfield's journey. Mayfield's always found a way to back it up on the field, and that makes everything else he brings to the table that much more impactful.

"One thing I know about him: he walk it like he talk it," Browns wide receiver Jarvis Landry said. "That's something that I appreciate and respect about him, and he's continued to do that."

Browns wideout Jarvis Landry has said he respects Baker Mayfield because "he walk it like he talk it." Clearly, the admiration goes both ways.

No matter how accomplished the player, there's one rule that never wavers at the NFL Combine. If you played on the same team as one of the top quarterbacks in the draft, you're going to have to answer questions about him. That applies behind closed doors with NFL teams and in front of the cameras with media members.

One by one, Mayfield's teammates tried their best to express what his presence meant during a three-year stretch in which the Sooners won three Big 12 titles, made two College Football Playoff appearances, and lost just six times when Mayfield started. It went beyond the winning, the records he broke, the dance moves he displayed on more than one occasion.

"He's not who you think he is on the field and off the field. He's a captain. He's a leader. He's very focused," said Mayfield's left tackle at Oklahoma, Orlando Brown. "He's gonna bring everyone together and do what he needs to do."

Wide receiver Dede Westbrook, a teammate of Mayfield's from 2015 to '16, took it one step further in a November 2017 essay for The Players Tribune, a platform that let him expound on the impact Mayfield had on him while dispelling the negative narratives surrounding the polarizing quarterback. Mayfield drove Westbrook to practice every day despite Westbrook living 30 minutes from Oklahoma's practice fields. When the Sooners lost to Clemson in Mayfield's first trip to the College Football Playoff, Westbrook recalled a moment in the locker room when

With his "Pied Piper" mentality, Baker Mayfield came into the Browns locker room and immediately began changing its culture with his leadership and fiery personality.

Mayfield stood up and took accountability for every part of Oklahoma's lopsided defeat.

"He was a leader in our locker room, *the* leader in our huddle, and probably the hardest working guy at practice," Westbrook wrote for The Players Tribune. "I wish I had some weird secret to tell you about Baker, honestly. Like that he picked his nose or was mean to servers in restaurants—something to show you that the guy is human like the rest of us. But that's just not him at all. Baker's a winner, plain and simple. He might not even be human for all I know."

* * *

Mayfield had the Browns at "hee hee."

That was the moment Hue Jackson saw Mayfield as the "Pied Piper" of Oklahoma football. It took a simple noise—"hee hee"—for Mayfield to get the attention of his teammates, who flocked around him as he began his pre-draft workout with Jackson and the rest of Cleveland's executives. The draw to Mayfield went beyond his on-field skills and canceled out the perceived flaws—height, track record of Big 12 quarterbacks, and a few regrettable moments during his college career. It was the whole package that had to be seen and experienced to truly appreciate.

"This guy is as good of a quarterback going out statistically that there has been," Jackson said. "You take the other characteristics that we look for in leadership, getting guys to play, and the hunger and the desire to be

Browns wide receiver Antonio Callaway was on the receiving end of history when he caught Baker Mayfield's 24th touchdown pass of his season in the Week 17 finale against the Baltimore Ravens, which was the most-ever for a rookie quarterback.

the best, there is no question that it all added up for us."

Mayfield made a fast impression on his new teammates, some of whom were more than 10 years older. He took ownership of the second-team offense he led throughout the preseason and displayed the same kind of fun-loving, borderline laid-back demeanor whenever players surrounded him in the huddle. When the season began, Mayfield blended in and prepared as if he were the starter. And when his time arrived in the second quarter of Cleveland's must-win game against the Jets, Mayfield promptly showed how comfortable he was in his own skin, engaging in some trash talk with an opposing linebacker as he entered the huddle for the first time.

"I was like, 'All right Baker,'" veteran offensive lineman Joel Bitonio said. "Second half, Baker came out and led us to victory. So he backed up his talk."

That kind of chatter, followed by the appropriate actions, fell exactly into Mayfield's plans to help change the culture inside the Browns locker room. He wasn't around for the previous two seasons, when Cleveland won just once in 32 tries, and he never pretended to be. But he knew he'd be counting on many who had experienced every last one of those losses. At any mention of the past or specifically "0–16," Mayfield would be quick to point out this was a new year and a brand-new team. He saw the talent general manager John Dorsey stockpiled in his first offseason with the team, and he knew it was capable of doing more than just "competing." This was a group Mayfield believed could win and win regularly.

It was just on him, as a leader—whenever that opportunity arose—to get the most out of the players who surrounded him just like he did at every other stage of his career.

"If you can elevate the level of play of your teammates around you—and not just the 10 guys around you and on the field at the same time, but the defense and the special teams and even the coaches—if you can inspire and get people to play with a passion and a focus that they didn't have before, that is the most important thing," Mayfield said. "If you can get guys to believe it and never have a doubt, no matter what the score is or what your record is, you can start something great."

The Browns were showing just that Week 12 against the Bengals, easily the team's most convincing win of the season, and Mayfield was at the center of it both during and after the final whistle. The postgame handshake with Jackson, followed by a controversial Instagram comment, elicited plenty of strong, negative reactions from national pundits.

Mayfield took it head on, answering question after question about the situation

The way Baker Mayfield carried himself on the field galvanized his teammates, like running back Nick Chubb, who said "the whole team has his back."

"I'm never trying to be anybody else. I'm going to be the best version of myself. That's what has got me here."

—BAKER MAYFIELD

while stressing he would never be a "cookie-cutter quarterback."

"People get maturity confused with me being 100 percent comfortable in my own skin," Mayfield said. "That is absolutely how I am. I've always been that way. It's not immature. It's me being exactly who I am every day, being that same guy for our team, and I think that's very important for us right now.

"I'm never trying to be anybody else. I'm going to be the best version of myself. That's what has got me here."

One by one, just like at the Combine, the players around Mayfield inside the Browns locker room had his back. That's all that mattered.

"That's been his personality. Nobody is trying to stop that. We're actually encouraging him to be himself all of the time," Landry said. "For us, we don't have a problem with it. We stand behind him. That's our quarterback. He's our quarterback."

It goes both ways, and Mayfield had one of his finest leadership moments during one of the toughest for Browns fans to stomach. Trailing by 19 early in the second half Week 13 at Houston, Mayfield connected on what he thought was a 75-yard touchdown pass with Antonio Callaway. A holding call nullified the score but somehow, two plays later, Mayfield found Callaway again for another big pass play. As Callaway trucked toward the end zone, Texans defender Justin Reid popped the ball loose inside the 5-yard line and Houston recovered. Mayfield was initially sprinting down the field to congratulate Callaway, but, instead, he was there to console the rookie.

"It means everything," Callaway said. "I told you: he's the leader, the leader of the offense."

Callaway would go on to catch two of the most important passes from Mayfield during the season's final month. He was the wide receiver Mayfield spotted with a

From the first moment he took the field, Baker Mayfield commanded the Browns huddle with confidence and poise.

safety guarding him late Week 15 at Denver, inspiring an audible that resulted in what would become the game-winning touchdown. And in Cleveland's season finale at Baltimore, Callaway was on the receiving of history when Mayfield fired his 27th touchdown pass, giving him the most-ever by a rookie quarterback.

Even from a big personality like Mayfield, it's the little things that make all the difference.

"His leadership—especially as a rookie coming in—it's so genuine," Browns veteran center JC Tretter said. "People want to be around him; people gravitate toward him. And that's big because you gotta take a big step being a rookie in the locker room as well as leading older, veteran players. It's one of those things if you push too hard, if you are deemed fake, then people are gonna push back on you, but Baker's such a natural leader, such a genuine good person, it's made it easy to have older guys kinda gravitate toward him, work with and be excited to play with him."

* * *

During the Browns' Week 7 loss to the Buccaneers, Mayfield broke out for his longest run of the season, dashing down the middle of the field for 35 yards. He ended it with a customary quarterback slide to avoid a punishing hit, but one came his way anyways. Buccaneers safety Jordan

Whitehead dove at Mayfield, clipping him in the head and somehow avoiding a penalty in the process. Mayfield stood up, briefly got in Whitehead's face, and then ran back toward his teammates.

One day later, when the team converged to watch film, the feeling hit hard with Mayfield's teammates. Their quarterback got rocked, and not only did he get right back up, but he also let the defender know it'd take more than that to slow him down.

Nine weeks later, when Mayfield took a similarly questionable late hit on a fourth quarter scramble against the Bengals, those same teammates showed their appreciation in an instant. As Carlos Dunlap sent Mayfield tumbling out of bounds, a horde of Browns teammates, led by veteran receiver Jarvis Landry, jumped into the fray and confronted Dunlap.

It was a small but powerful moment, as the Browns made it clear they had Mayfield's back.

"You've got to protect Baker. You've got to keep him safe and playing at a high level. The whole team has his back," running back Nick Chubb said. "It doesn't matter who it was, everyone would have run over there and fought for the Browns. We are a family now and we play for each other." ♦

Former Browns quarterback Bernie Kosar presented Baker Mayfield with the Athlete of the Year Award at the Cleveland Sports Awards in February 2019.

Right QB, Right Franchise

Perhaps the biggest impact Baker Mayfield made during his breakout rookie season can be found in the heart of Cleveland's Warehouse District.

For years—too many, in the eyes of most Browns fans—The Jersey hung inside the window of Brokaw Inc., a small advertising agency on Cleveland's popular West 6th Street. It was a traditional Browns road white jersey draped on a female mannequin, whose back faced the street, but it featured a sordid twist.

The Jersey, before Brokaw Inc., took some creative license with it, was one of the most popular in the Browns' rich history, so popular you'll still see more than a handful of them on game days throughout FirstEnergy Stadium. The No. 2 Tim Couch jersey, which hit the shelves after the 1999 NFL Draft, was the unofficial shirt choice for thousands and thousands of Browns fans who were not only thrilled to have their team back after it was taken from them four years earlier, but also believed they had the young quarterback who could one day lead them to their first Super Bowl.

It didn't work out that way, of course. Couch was out of the league after five seasons, battered and bruised after playing behind a patchwork offensive line for most of his time in Cleveland. The Browns would have to go back to the drawing board to find their future, long-term quarterback, something they hadn't had since Bernie Kosar took the city by storm in the 1980s.

They tried and tried and tried, and The Jersey was there to document every single swing at the plate. Everyone was treated the same, whether it be first-round picks

Baker Mayfield, still sporting his offseason beard, and fiancée Emily Wilkinson walked the red carpet prior to the 2019 Kentucky Derby.

When Mayfield took the first snap Week 4 at Oakland, he became the 30th different quarterback since 1999 to start for the Browns.

Brady Quinn, Brandon Weeden, and Johnny Manziel; journeymen like Doug Pederson, Kelly Holcomb, and Josh McCown; or off-the-radar backups who were thrust into the spotlight because of injuries and other misfortunes like Spergon Wynn, Austin Davis. and Kevin Hogan. The names hung on pieces of paper to the bottom right of "Couch," which was crossed out with marker. When a new name emerged, the one above it got the same treatment.

This carried on for nearly 20 years, save for a stretch in 2016 when The Jersey was briefly retired in the spirit of good karma following the Cleveland Cavaliers' magical NBA Finals victory. When Mayfield took the first snap Week 4 at Oakland, he became the 30th different quarterback since 1999 to start for the Browns.

Months later, as Cleveland wrapped up its seventh and final win of the season,

The Jersey was no more. A No. 6 Mayfield jersey—the Color Rush one he sported the night of his magical debut—hung in its place. A few blocks down the street on the shores of Lake Erie, Mayfield stood at midfield and addressed what remained of a sellout crowd.

"It's a team game," Mayfield said, "and you're a part of it."

* * *

It wasn't love at first sight between Mayfield and all segments of the Browns fan base.

There were plenty of fans who cheer for the Browns on Sundays and the Ohio State Buckeyes on Saturdays who were still outraged by Mayfield planting the Oklahoma flag in the center of OSU's "Block O." There were also those who hitched all their pre-draft support to one of the other highly touted quarterbacks. Chronicling the successes of

In an NFL combine media appearance, Baker Mayfield vowed to end the ever-growing list of Browns starting quarterback names on the back of The Jersey.

Baker Mayfield donned his cleats reading WOKE UP FEELING DANGEROUS *prior to the Browns' Week 14 game against the Carolina Panthers.*

Mayfield offered hope, a promise that better days were right around the corner if he were chosen to be the team's franchise quarterback.

players Cleveland could have selected in the draft is a commonly practiced, anguish-filled exercise performed regularly by Browns fans, and many feared they'd be doing the same with the other signal-callers for the next decade. One Cleveland radio personality was so adamant about the other quarterbacks, he vowed to eat horse manure if the Browns selected Mayfield.

And then there were those who couldn't look at Mayfield without seeing Manziel, the team's most recent first-round failure. Similarly undersized, Manziel took the college football world by storm as an instant star at Texas A&M, won the 2012 Heisman Trophy, and entered the NFL Draft one year later. The Browns selected him with the 22nd pick in the 2014 draft, evoking a level of excitement from their fan base that hadn't been seen since Couch was picked. That moment was ultimately the peak of Manziel's time in Cleveland, as he struggled with issues on and off the field for two seasons before he was released.

Mayfield bristled at these comparisons, because he knew they weren't anything close to true. He understood the apprehension, though, and took the endless queries in stride as he went through the grind of the pre-draft process.

"People forget he was a talented football player, first things first, before he got caught up in whatever it was. Talented football player," Mayfield said at the Combine. "But when it comes to that comparison...we're two completely different people. He's said it, I've said it. When it comes down to it, I'll do anything to play this game and I'll do everything to keep playing it."

Mayfield did his homework on the Browns. He couldn't feel what the fans felt through two decades that produced just one playoff appearance or through two of the most recent seasons that produced just one win, so he never pretended to. Instead, he offered hope, a promise that better days were right around the corner if he were chosen to be the team's franchise quarterback.

Baker Mayfield chided Browns fans when attendance was light for the Week 14 game against the Carolina Panthers. As a result, in Cleveland's home finale two weeks later, the fans sold out the stadium, with thematic signs in tow.

By the time he arrived at the Combine, he knew there was a special set of circumstances that came with being the No. 1 pick. It wasn't just the pressure that comes with the title. It was the location, the position he played, the responsibility. Mayfield, as he proved time and again throughout his high school and college careers, liked a challenge. He could have gone places where it would have been much easier to land a starting job just like he could have very well preferred to land somewhere else on Draft Day.

That just wasn't how Mayfield was wired.

"It is a mentality," Mayfield said. "You come in and think about the past so that you can focus on the present and work for the future. For Cleveland right now, we are making the right moves. Tyrod [Taylor] and I, we are going to put an end to that list of the QB names on the back of the jersey."

The Browns look to blossom with Baker Mayfield under center, forming a relationship the city of Cleveland can enjoy for years.

"We are becoming a team that is prideful of playing at home and protecting our territory. We would love to have more fan support."

—BAKER MAYFIELD IN A LATE 2018 GAME

* * *

Couch liked the Browns' plans to let Mayfield begin his career on the sidelines as Taylor's backup. That was the plan for Couch, too, but it was scrapped after one game. No matter how ready the quarterback is, the clock starts the moment the player viewed as the franchise's future steps onto the field, and Couch knew this better than most.

"With Baker coming in as the No. 1 pick, people think this is the guy that's going to turn around the franchise and finally solve the quarterback issue they've had here for a long time," Couch said in July 2018 during his first visit back to the Browns facility since his career came to an end.

"That's a lot of pressure for a young guy to deal with."

Mayfield just wasn't your typical young guy.

He seized the opportunity when it presented itself that fateful night against the Jets and never looked back. Even as the No.

1 pick, Mayfield never removed the chip on his shoulder. If anything, it grew even larger while representing a city that carries itself with a similar edge—tired of the same old jokes, frisky and comfortable as an underdog, indelibly proud of what it is and where it's going.

Mayfield fed off every bit of it.

"When you have that support, when you have people that have those shirts, those sayings, and you wake up and you see those people wearing those shirts and say those things when you are on the streets, it makes it fun," Mayfield said. "It makes it feel like this is a whole team effort, which it is."

Near the end of his first season, Mayfield was even comfortable enough to step into what is typically a no-go zone with Cleveland sports fans. After a dazzling comeback win over the Panthers in Week 14, Mayfield poked at Browns fans for leaving a few too many orange seats empty. Never mind this was a fan base that weathered the storm of 0–16 and

"I relate to Cleveland. The work ethic, the stuff that you have to earn it around here, that is what the Browns are all about."

—BAKER MAYFIELD

1–15 the past two seasons; never mind it was the time of year when the wind swirls extra hard off Lake Erie. Mayfield wanted the house full when the team returned in two weeks for its home finale against the Bengals.

"We are becoming a team that is prideful of playing at home and protecting our territory. We would love to have more fan support," Mayfield said. "Today was cold, I get it, but having more people, especially at our last home game coming up, we would love to have more people in the stands cheering for us because we feed off of the energy."

Comments like these would have drawn backlash from any number of other Cleveland athletes, but from Mayfield, they were heard as a rallying cry. It was Mayfield flexing the "Pied Piper" muscles he had at Oklahoma. In the previous season's home finale, the Browns barely filled half of the seats for their final home game. One year later, even though the Browns were officially eliminated from the

playoff hunt the night before the game, fans filled every last seat in a game that turned into a party by the end of the first half.

Mayfield grew up 1,400 miles away from downtown Cleveland, but you could have fooled anyone who watched him take the city by storm as a 23-year-old rookie. He embodied everything Browns fans and Clevelanders are all about and, most importantly, was proud to do it.

The Jersey says it all.

"It's not always pretty, but you go through the good times and the bad times together," Mayfield said. "There has been a lot more good than bad as of recent. It is fun. I expect that relationship to continue to grow. I relate to Cleveland. The work ethic, the stuff that you have to earn it around here, that is what the Browns are all about.

"It's going to be a good relationship for a long time." ♦

Mayfield's first name has provided no shortage of creative fan tributes and signage.

More Than a Quarterback

Baker Mayfield turned lemons into lemonade with the tap of his finger.

The rookie quarterback was fined by the NFL for a gesture he made on the sideline during Cleveland's home finale against the Bengals. Browns fans disagreed, and a movement began on social media. A GoFundMe page titled "Pay Baker's Fine" popped up, and the donations poured in.

Mayfield spotted the campaign a few days after his rookie season came to an end. He didn't need the money, of course, and the fine was ultimately reduced to just $1,700 after an appeal. Still, there was good to be done. Mayfield sent out his first tweet in more than a week, reaching a following of more than 515,000 and urging fans to donate because the money would instead be sent to Providence House, a Cleveland-based crisis nursery that provides emergency shelter and care for children in crisis who are at risk of abuse or neglect while offering family support services to strengthen and stabilize families.

In just a few weeks, more than $5,400 was raised for a charity near and dear to Mayfield's heart. It was a small moment, nowhere close to the other types of charitable donations he's been associated with since entering the NFL, but it symbolized the effectiveness in which Mayfield has turned his exponentially growing celebrity platform—thanks to a combination of shrewd marketing, his likeability and, of course, incredible performances on the field—into one that positively affects the less fortunate.

★ ★ ★

Mayfield spent the summer before his senior season at Oklahoma plowing through 35 hours of community service. The

Cleveland Browns fans have enjoyed learning about who Baker Mayfield is off the field almost as much as learning about who he is when he's playing for their team.

experience left a lasting impact, as Mayfield saw firsthand the power of giving back as he worked with Meals on Wheels, Special Olympics, and other charities around the Norman, Oklahoma, area.

"I think I've truly been able to make a difference, and it's made a difference in me, that I can go out and help. I get true joy out of that, being able to help people," Mayfield told reporters at Big 12 Media Day, according to the *Tulsa World*.

"No matter what I think is going on, I'm very blessed in the situation I'm at. I've been given a lot, and I'm fortunate to be in the spot, in the position, I'm in."

Mayfield simply had to be himself to leave an everlasting impact on young Mackenzie Asher, an 11-year-old girl who was suffering from acute myeloid leukemia. By the time she met Mayfield before Oklahoma's September 2017 game against Tulane as part of the Sooners' Special Spectators program, she'd

Above: Passionate Browns fans started a GoFundMe to pay a Baker Mayfield fine at the end of his rookie season. He galvanized his Twitter followers to raise more than $5,000 and redirected the funds to Providence House, a Cleveland-based organization close to his heart. Opposite: Baker Mayfield and popular gamer Ninja presented the Best Celebration award at the eighth annual NFL Honors ceremony in February 2019.

"No matter what I think is going on, I'm very blessed in the situation I'm at. I've been given a lot, and I'm fortunate to be in the spot, in the position, I'm in."

—Baker Mayfield

undergone a seven-month hospital stay only to find out months later the cancer had returned.

All the adversity didn't take one smidge out of Asher's bubbly personality, and that was apparent to Mayfield throughout her visit. In an ESPN feature, Asher's father Jayson said the bond between Mayfield and his daughter was a "connection that surprised us all."

"She had a smile on her face no matter what," Mayfield told ESPN's Tom Rinaldi in a feature that aired before Oklahoma's trip to the 2018 Rose Bowl. "She found a way to have happiness."

Asher lost her battle with cancer just a couple of days before Mayfield was named the 2017 Heisman Trophy winner. Mayfield discussed the impact she made on him in a pre-ceremony interview and spoke a few days later at Asher's funeral, where he said the Sooners would be dedicating the rest of their season to her.

"I've been fortunate enough to be on a platform where I get to meet special people, people that have impacted lives, but I've never fell for someone as fast as I have for Mackenzie," Mayfield said at the funeral. "Her smile is infectious, her heart, her bravery, her courage, you can tell it's 100 percent genuine all the time. That's something I like to pride myself on, but it will never compare to her."

* * *

Mayfield entered the pre-draft process as one of the highest-profile members of the 2018 class. It grew even larger in the build-up to the draft, as Mayfield took fans behind the scenes throughout his journey in a nine-part web

Cleveland fans may be alarmed to see Baker Mayfield sporting Milwaukee Brewers gear, but he's supporting his good friend, right fielder Christian Yelich.

series called *Behind Baker*. From his whirlwind week at the Super Bowl, to the workouts he went through before the NFL Combine, to the endless flights he made for all of his pre-draft meetings with teams, to the makings of his instantly viral tribute to Brett Favre the night before the draft, Mayfield showed it all to those who wanted to follow along the journey.

There were plenty who did, and they learned just how much went into Mayfield's improbable rise to the No. 1 pick. And for those who missed it, an adapted version of the series that focused heavily on Mayfield's backstory, *All the Way Up: Baker Mayfield*, ran in four parts on FOX leading up to Mayfield's first training camp with the Browns.

"I wanted a little more of an inside look. There is a lot more work and whatnot that comes with it than people know. Just a little insight," Mayfield said. "My story has always been a little different, so giving them a little twist on it."

Even before he took a single snap with the Browns, Mayfield was a hot commodity in the marketing world. He signed endorsement deals with Nike, Panini America, Bose, and a slew of others by late May 2018, according to Crain's Cleveland Business. That's customary for a No. 1 pick in the draft. What truly catapulted Mayfield into the limelight was his performance on the field during a season that ended with him voted

Make no mistake, Baker Mayfield, who attended the Indians game against the Blue Jays in April 2019, still shows love to his fellow Cleveland athletes.

as the Pro Football Writers of America Rookie of the Year. Each highlight-filled week along the way validated the Browns not only had a star-in-the-making at quarterback, but also a high-profile one. He won the NFL's fan-voted Rookie of the Week seven of the eight times he was nominated, taking home the honor even after games he lost or produced stat lines that didn't match some of his competition. Mayfield's sky-high popularity was at its peak in Northeast Ohio, but it resonated nationally on a level few Browns players have ever achieved—and that was just after one season in the NFL. By the end of the season, Mayfield's jersey was the seventh-best seller—fourth-best among quarterbacks—from the official NFLShop. Of the top 10, Mayfield was the only player who didn't make the Pro Bowl and was one of two from teams that didn't finish with a winning record.

Even with the Browns coming up just short of the playoffs, Mayfield stayed plenty busy to kick off his first NFL offseason. He rubbed his face on an emu during a game of "Nuzzle Whaaa?" on *The Late Late Show with James Corden*, hopped into the cold tub for a one-on-one interview with comedian Kevin Hart, taped a "Baking with Baker" segment alongside Cooper Manning for FOX's NFC Championship pregame show, went through a second year of stops on Radio Row at the Super Bowl LIII, dined with NFL

The future is bright in Cleveland. Superstar wideout Odell Beckham, Jr. joined Mayfield, Myles Garrett (left) and Jarvis Landry on the Browns in the 2019 offseason.

In his eyes, he's a football player first and foremost. Everything else comes second.

superstars Von Miller and Odell Beckham Jr., and presented "Best Celebration" alongside video gaming icon Ninja at NFL Honors. At one point in the month, Mayfield shot his part in the NFL's instant classic Super Bowl commercial, which launched the league's NFL100 campaign. As a football game breaks out in a ballroom, legendary Patriots quarterback Tom Brady hands off all his Super Bowl rings to Mayfield, who encourages the six-time Super Bowl champion by saying, "Get out there, old man." Browns fans certainly dug the symbolism, seeing it as a passing-of-the-torch moment between the quarterbacks.

Mayfield shook his head when he was asked about his celebrity status in a February interview with reporters after he took home "Professional Athlete of the Year" at the Greater Cleveland Sports Awards. In his eyes, he's a football player first and foremost. Everything else comes second.

"I'm not that at all," Mayfield said. "I just get to enjoy the time because I think it's important to step away from the game for a little bit, do some fun things here and there, be around different athletes, but when it's time to train, I'll be able to shut that off and go do that. That's something I pride myself on."

* * *

One of Mayfield's finest moments as a rookie was a spur-of-the-moment decision.

A little more than a month removed from partnering with Barstool Sports on a clothing line that would donate 100 percent of its proceeds to Special Olympics in Greater Cleveland, Mayfield took his seat at the Providence House 23rd annual Deck the House Auction Benefit. When it was time to auction off a dinner for two with Mayfield and his fiancée Emily Wilkinson, Mayfield didn't just take the stage; he took over the room,

Though he began the Browns' offseason organized team activity sessions with his offseason beard, Mayfield shaved shortly thereafter in preparation for his summer wedding to Emily Wilkinson.

"To be able to give back to a city that's believed in me and supported me, and to be able to impact the youth and give every kid a chance and have the same opportunities as everyone else, that's the important thing about it."

—BAKER MAYFIELD DURING THE WEEK OF SUPER BOWL LIII

microphone in hand, as he playfully prodded everyone in the room to increase their bids.

"Who's got the deep pockets in here? Green sweater, I see you," Mayfield said.

In the heat of the bidding, Mayfield doubled down, offering the dinner experience to multiple bidders. By the end, two separate groups donated more than $40,000 apiece.

Forget the 3,725 passing yards, by far the most ever by a Browns rookie. Forget the NFL-record 27 touchdown passes. Forget the 106.2 quarterback rating he posted in the second half of the season. In that moment, none of it mattered as much as the impact Mayfield had just made by embracing and maximizing

the massive platform he holds as the NFL's newest star quarterback.

"To be able to have that opportunity is very special," Mayfield said in a Super Bowl LIII appearance on *The Jim Rome Show*.

"To be able to give back to a city that's believed in me and supported me, and to be able to impact the youth and give every kid a chance and have the same opportunities as everyone else, that's the important thing about it.

"I don't want any of the credit, but I want those kids to have the same chance I did." ◆

Baker Mayfield was all smiles after his Browns defeated the Atlanta Falcons in Cleveland 28-16 on Sunday, November 11, 2018.

In a high-stakes, primetime Week 15 showdown on December 15, 2018, Baker Mayfield led the Browns over the Denver Broncos 17–16 in one of his best games of the season.

Baker Mayfield, his teammates, and the Browns fan base were all ecstatic after the team fought its way back from a 14-point deficit to defeat the New York Jets 21–17 in Mayfield's NFL debut, Week 3 of the 2018 season.